THE WONDERFUL WACKY WORLD
OF
MARKETINGMOBILES

PROMOTIONAL VEHICLES OF THE WORLD

JAMES HALE

This book is dedicated to my brother William.

VELOCE PUBLISHING
THE PUBLISHER OF FINE AUTOMOTIVE BOOKS

Also from Veloce Publishing -

First published September 2005 by Veloce Publishing Limited, 33 Trinity Street, Dorchester DT1 1TT, England. Fax 01305 268864/e-mail info@veloce.co.uk/web www.veloce.co.uk or www.velocebooks.com
ISBN 1-84584-003-8/UPC 781845-84003-7
Readers with ideas for automotive books, or books on other transport or related hobby subjects, are invited to write to the editorial director of Veloce Publishing at the above address.
British Library Cataloguing in Publication Data - A catalogue record for this book is available from the British Library. Typesetting, design and page make-up all by Veloce Publishing Ltd on Apple Mac. Printed in Malta by Gutenberg.

THE WONDERFUL WACKY WORLD

OF

MARKETINGMOBILES

PROMOTIONAL VEHICLES OF THE WORLD

JAMES HALE

Contents

The **GUINNESS®** beer brand was promoted by this figurine on top of the company's export delivery vehicles in the early 1960s. (Diageo. The word 'GUINNESS' and the HARP device are trade marks)

About the author

James Hale was born on England's south coast, and has lived in Brighton – the 'city by the sea' – for the last 25 years. After graduating from art college, he developed a career in marketing and public relations, whilst also working as a freelance automotive writer and photographer. James has been photographing and writing about unusual vehicles for more than 20 years, and has a keen interest in everything from military vehicles to fun cars of the 1960s and 1970s, film cars and hot rods. He has worked regularly for major magazines including *VW Trends, Volksworld, VW Motoring, Ultra VW* and *Kit Car Magazine*, and has also written technical books on modifying the VW Beetle and VW Bus suspension, brakes and chassis for high performance, also published by Veloce.

James is the world's leading authority on dune buggies, owns the world's largest collection of toy buggies, and has written five books covering the buggy scene worldwide. He has regularly appeared in magazines and on TV and radio to talk about his passion for these cute and irreverent fun vehicles. This MarketingMobiles book combines his professional interest in marketing and promotion with some of the most oddball vehicles ever to be driven on public highways.

James is a member of The Society of Automotive Historians, The Bureau of Freelance Photographers, and an associate of the Guild of Motoring Writers. This is his seventh book for Veloce Publishing.

Built in 1923 on a standard 30hp Daimler car chassis, this Worthington's bottle van was used to promote White Shield India Pale Ale whilst delivering advertising materials to pubs during the 1920s and '30s. It is seen here at the Montagu Motor Museum in the late 1950s, after it was replaced by the brewer. (Motoring Picture Library, Beaulieu)

Acknowledgements

The author and publisher are indebted to the following for the provision of photographs and other assistance, without which this book would not have been possible: George W Green; Giles Chapman; Peter Rhodes; Robin Wager; Paul Wager; Neil Birkitt; Roland Swälas; Glenn Björk; Tom Torrans; Nick Baldwin; Pastor Robert Dunlop; Jon Day, Beaulieu Motoring Picture Library; Sam Turner, Ludvigsen Library; Colin Samways, Cadbury World; Dick London, Cadbury Schweppes Plc; Lisa McElhinney, Diageo Archive; Carina Badger, GUINNESS IP; Catherine Lister, Coors Visitor Centre & the Museum of Brewing; Annesietske Stapel, Heineken Experience; Jim Orr, Benson Ford Research Center – The Henry Ford; Ryan Morton, American Truck Historical Society; Jon Bill, Auburn Cord Duesenberg Museum; Jane Griffin, MTR Promotions Ltd; *Custom Car*; Getty Images; Classicphotos; Reuters; Auto Archive; Fran at Innocent Drinks.

All photographs in this book have been credited, where known, to the original photographer, magazine or copyright holder. Where this has not been possible, credit is given to the collection owner.

Outspan commissioned six of these novel advertising vehicles, based on the versatile Mini, between 1972 and 1974. They were extensively used in advertising campaigns in the UK, France, and Germany, and one is still in use in South Africa. The high centre of gravity limited speed to 30mph, and prevented over-enthusiastic braking to preclude the vehicle from rolling over. (*Custom Car*)

Foreword

My earliest recollection of visiting a motoring museum is during a trip to the New Forest to see the newly opened National Motoring Museum at Beaulieu in 1972. Whilst others may have been in awe of the displays of sleek classic racing cars, the earliest veteran or vintage vehicles, or the awesome, powerful land speed record cars, I was entranced by a few quirky promotional vehicles on show: I particularly remember a car shaped like an Outspan orange, and a lorry fashioned like a beer bottle. They were different in a captivating sort of way and immediately spoke volumes to me about the ingenuity of product advertising. This wasn't just a case of simply sign-writing a flat-sided van, but creating a facsimile of the product itself in a larger-than-life, mobile form. The phrase 'it does what it says on the tin' hadn't been invented then but, if it had, it would have summed up my exact feelings for the way the vehicles promoted the products they represented. As I stared at them, spellbound, little did I know then that, years later, I would write about these exact same vehicles, and many others like them.

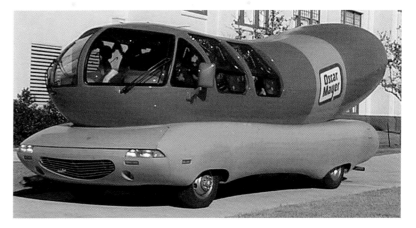

The Oscar Mayer Wienermobile™ is a familiar sight in the US, promoting Yellow Band hot dogs and luncheon meats. This is one of eight productmobiles in today's fleet owned by Kraft Foods, and is based on a GMC W Series truck chassis. Designed originally in 1931, with a 13-foot metal hot dog, the vehicles have evolved through the years and now feature glassfibre bodies. (Oscar Meyer Division, Kraft Foods)

Cadbury Creme Egg cars were built to promote the fondant-filled chocolate eggs at Cadbury World in Bournville, and at events around Britain, during the key selling season between New Year and Easter. Drivers entered the cars through gull-wing doors at the side of the egg-shaped, glassfibre bodies which were mounted on 1988/89 Bedford Rascal van chassis. (Cadbury Schweppes plc/V4 Design Studio)

A career in marketing only heightened my interest in anything to do with product promotion. The idea of 'marketingmobiles' (or 'productmobiles' as they are also known) never left me, and the more I came to look into the subject, the more I realised they had never been done adequate justice in print. After all, there are books covering just about every other type of vehicle, so why not promotional vehicles?

Researching and writing this book is my attempt at redressing the balance. A lot of very understanding people helped me along the way. I use the word 'understanding' advisedly ... This was never going to be the easiest subject to delve into, and to those

who tuned into the off-beat wavelength on which I operated for a year or two, and helped me considerably, I thank you. A special mention goes to George Green who encouraged me enormously, helped me with photos, and whose book *Special Use Vehicles* helped light the way when the going got tough.

Next time you see a promotional vehicle at a display or event, remember to stop and look, smile, and then buy the product it's advertising. If you do that, you will have made a hard-working product manager very happy.

James Hale
Brighton, England

So popular have productmobiles been in the UK that even children's toy versions of the vehicles have been produced. The diminutive items shown here replicate the famous red telephone on wheels for Direct Line Insurance, an Outspan orange car, and a Cadbury's Creme Egg car.

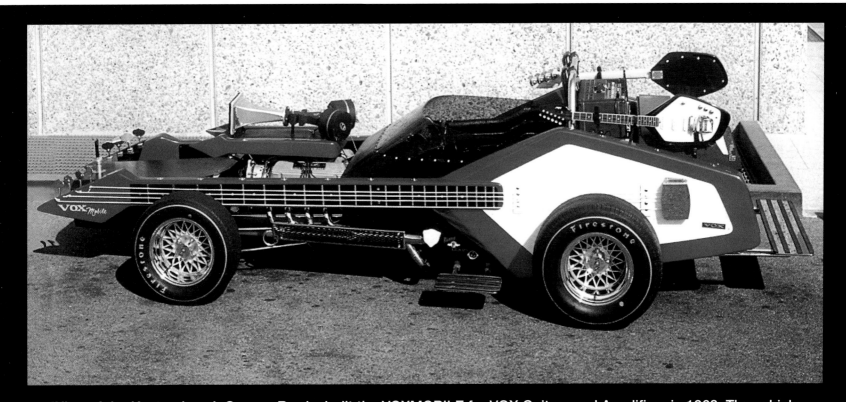

'King of the Kustomizers', George Barris, built the VOXMOBILE for VOX Guitars and Amplifiers in 1968. The vehicle resembles a classic 1960s VOX guitar in profile, and can create its own high-fidelity audio through the use of self-contained VOX sound equipment. An entire rock 'n roll band can plug in and play through its amplifiers, with a power output of close to 1000 watts! (George Barris)

In 1910 the American Thermos Bottle Company promoted its unique Thermos flask by creating a large motorised replica. With an aluminium body shaped like the Model 24 flask, and a mahogany interior for the driver and passengers, the vehicle toured the country to promote the product – the perfect accompaniment to any picnic. Carrying the slogan: 'It's a Thermos or just a vacuum bottle' on the sides, and 'Keeps Hot – keeps Cold' on the wheels, the vehicle made an appearance at the 1924 Democratic Convention in New York. (King-Seeley Co/George W Green)

Introduction

At the beginning of the 20th century, motorised transportation was a new and developing trend that would quickly become an integral and indispensable part of the modern world. The earliest vehicles, whilst powered by internal combustion engines, still had much in common with designs from the era of horse drawn carriages. This would soon change as the motor car evolved from being a novelty plaything for the wealthy, to providing a flexible means of transportation for the masses.

The first cars were the products of coachbuilders and were expensive, craft-built designs. In the US, Henry Ford changed that by using mass-production techniques in motor car production.

His earliest vehicles date back to 1896, but it was in the early years of the 20th century that he achieved his dream of 'a motorcar for the great multitude' with the introduction of the Model T. With cheap vehicles finally a reality, it was not long before passenger cars and trucks began to appear in increasing numbers on the expanding road network.

With perhaps a certain inevitability, those involved in commerce recognised the unrivalled opportunity to advertise their services or products on the sides of the vehicles. Such 'rolling billboards' were an ideal method of taking advertising messages out to wider audiences in towns and cities. The true

The inter-war years saw the development of a large number of consumer products, as well as interesting vehicles to promote them. This giant 'toothpaste tube' was built by Aldgate & City Motors in Britain in the early 1930s to advertise Kolynos dental cream. Billed as an antiseptic dental cream, the American product helped eliminate 'bacterial mouth' – a condition as bad as it sounded, and a ticket ultimately for false teeth. The Kolynos brand was eventually acquired by Colgate-Palmolive. (Motoring Picture Library, Beaulieu)

development of the consumer age was yet to come, but these early beginnings were a tentative way for manufacturers and tradesmen to bring advertising to prospective customers by a new medium that created demand for their goods. In the US, during a period when sign-written advertising on vehicles was rapidly increasing, another trend was developing that would go a stage further in product promotion, sampling and demonstrations of both consumer and industrial goods.

A number of novelty vehicles were constructed with unusual bodies shaped like the actual product, but in a much larger form. Such visually exciting vehicles endorsed the association between the shape and design of the product in the mind of the consumer, and were aimed at increasing sales of the product in towns or at events where they were displayed or, later, when the buyer was choosing their purchases in a retail environment. These promotional vehicles were often referred to a 'productmobiles' and were useful in raising product awareness, aiding what would become termed 'product recall' on a subliminal level, which – it was believed – would result in longer term demand.

The uninhibited growth of vehicle ownership was checked by WWI in Europe. Following the cessation of hostilities in 1918, life began to return to normal in Britain, where vehicle technology was still rudimentary. The period between 1920 and 1930 saw little more than basic family cars, with Ford still a leader in the production of 'commonplace cars'. Some productmobiles appeared during this time, more often than not promoting consumables such as food or beer brands.

In the US the harsh economic climate of the Great Depression (1929-1941) took its toll and left the country with money and goods in short supply. Then, in 1939, a second European conflict was again to devastate and re-shape the world. By 1945

Ford cars have been put to many interesting uses, but this tiny travelling chapel of the Rev Branford Clarke, New York, is in a class of its own. His 'perambulatory pulpit', built in 1921 on a Ford Model T touring car chassis, was complete with collapsible steeple, stained glass windows, and a small organ – played by his wife – and was used to preach along Broadway in the years after the end of WWI. The Rev Mr Clarke became New York's famous 'poet-painter-preacher' when he illustrated his sermons with canvasses he painted himself. (From the collections of The Henry Ford)

The Paris Salon in the 1950s provided a showcase for the art of the commercial vehicle coachbuilder. This strange vehicle, built in 1949 to promote the Sofil brand, and shown at the 1952 exhibition by Carrosserie L Heukiez, is in the shape of a giant light bulb, and is based on a commercial vehicle chassis. This continental company developed its product range of lighting and entertainment by diversifying into the IT systems that it makes today.
(Redolfo Mailander/Ludvigsen Library)

As an advertising gimmick, Duckhams built a giant, three metre high oilcan called the 'Q Car' to attract attention at shows and public events. Built in 1969 on Mini underpinnings and powered by a 998cc engine, the wheelbase was shorter than the Mini by nearly 3ft, and was fitted with a Ford rear axle. The 'Q Car' livery was updated regularly to match the contemporary packaging used, and toured the country during the 1970s. Its first outing was a promotion at Woolco. In 1973, Duckhams contracted rally ace, Paddy Hopkirk, to feature in a five week television and press advertising campaign using the re-painted vehicle to promote a lubricating oil called 'New Formula Q', with a 'save money on motoring' theme, and backed by a 16-page giveaway magazine. (Motoring Picture Library, Beaulieu)

when peace finally resumed, WWII had left Europe shattered, and American ideology severely scarred. The British national austerity programme, with ration books enduring until late 1954, prevented the country from becoming fully mobile for many years. Consumerism was still but a dream, and advertising was confined to essential goods, affordable to a British public rebuilding broken lives and bombed-out landscapes.

Early signs of a future for cars and commercial vehicles came from the US where returning American servicemen – having witnessed the horrors of war – wanted to live their lives to the full. They wanted leisure, consumer goods – and cars. Automotive technology had been given a boost during the 1940s due to military developments, so the motor car was able to make a quantum leap forward in designs that would soon become motoring icons.

The dawn of the 1950s also saw the advent of a new species; the teenager. Rejecting conformist lives which they felt had resulted in the conflict, these new radicals embraced modern fashion, branded goods, television, rock and roll music, and the politics of peace. Such consumerism demand helped drive development of promotional vehicles in a world re-born after war.

In 1977, Mini owners could become part of a national advertising scheme to 'make their cars even more economical' by having them sign-written to promote manufacturers such as Levi's. Whilst not exactly resembling a pair of Levi's jeans, the zip motif on the side of this Mini – ably supported by the model in blue denim hot pants – is enough to suggest the Levi's brand in this period Leyland Cars advertisement. (Giles Chapman Library)

Whilst the earliest productmobiles tended to advertise consumables like food, confectionery and beverages, the new guard of advertising vehicles that appeared in postwar years generally promoted a more diverse range of products. Everything from sports goods to footwear, lighting equipment to cigarette lighters, cameras to musical equipment, and motoring accessories to industrial hardware began to appear. With each passing decade it has seemed that the widespread availability of advertising media on radio and TV, and more recently the Internet, might deplete the marketing value of these quirky productmobiles, but this has not been the case. New promotional vehicles continue to be built today and remain hugely popular wherever they appear, complementing other forms of advertising rather than being replaced by it. Interestingly, some of the earliest

advertising vehicles have even been re-created in recent years to tour public venues and events as part of an overall brand TV promotion.

Over the last 100 years the car has helped shape the modern world, for better or worse. As part of that worldwide development, advertising vehicles have left their mark wherever they have been used, and still continue to regularly appear on the world's highways. Who could fail to be impressed by a giant red hot dog, bright yellow peanut or pink stiletto shoe driving down the road? Whether providing a mobile demonstration and sales unit, or acting as an unforgettable aide memoir for shoppers on their next supermarket trip, the productmobile has a place in the hearts and minds of today's consumers. The world would be a poorer place without them; long may they continue!

Chapter 1: *Meals on wheels*

Promotional vehicles first came into being in the early 1900s with sign-written vans such as this early example advertising 'original and best' Carter's crisps of Kilburn. The flat sides of the van provided an ideal rolling billboard on which to display logos or messages advertising product and manufacturer.

By the mid-1920s, advertising vehicles became more sophisticated. Realising that engaging onlookers in some way would quickly draw a crowd, this 1926 Auburn Quaker Oats Company promotional vehicle used movement and sound as key elements to grab attention. A canon shot puffed wheat or rice into the gazebo at the rear of the car to symbolise the slogan 'Foods Shot from Guns'. (Auburn Cord Duesenberg Museum, Auburn, Indiana, USA)

UK drinks maker, Vimto, used a fleet of sign-written Albion and Ford delivery vans, built by Nichols & Co, to promote its 'ideal drink'. The Vimto fleet, and its drivers, are pictured here at the Ayres Road factory, Old Trafford, in 1928, prior to making its regular deliveries in the Manchester area.
(Motoring Picture Library, Beaulieu)

It wasn't long before delivery vans and trucks evolved into an exciting advertising concept by having bodywork shaped like a giant replica of the actual product. These revolutionary and visually exciting vehicles were called 'productmobiles' and helped manufacturers and distributors create considerable awareness of their goods with little additional outlay other than for the vehicle itself. In mid-1920s England, local baker, Mr Sillito, constructed a novelty bread delivery van with the driver's cab and van in the shape of loaves of bread. (Hulton Archive/ Topical Press Agency/ Getty Images)

The Owers bread van of the same period shows that more than one company benefited from the idea of using its loaf to sell more goods! The bread van was a perfect example of using the product shape to encourage identification amongst customers and generate sales. Now, if only they had been able to recreate the delicious aroma of freshly-baked bread, too ... (Nick Baldwin/Motoring Picture Library, Beaulieu)

Food and beverage manufacturers were some of the most prolific early users of productmobiles as a form of advertising, and are at the forefront of production of these unique vehicle designs to this day. This Absolom's Tea van, shaped like a giant teapot, was built on a Trojan chassis. Coachbuilding firm, A Crofts of Croydon, created the superb bodywork to promote Absolom's Golden Tips which, as the message on the side tells us, was pure black china tea, giving 288 cups to the pound. (Motoring Picture Library, Beaulieu)

The Absolom's Tea fleet used Trojan vehicles, though not all were like the unique teapot-shaped vehicle in the foreground. The Absolom's Golden Tips teapot would certainly have generated a lot of interest whilst out making deliveries or attending sales promotions at local stores. (Motoring Picture Library, Beaulieu)

A fruit importer's Ford lorry photographed in October 1928 in Covent Garden, London. Leaving no doubt about the trade of the owner, the driver's cab is fashioned in the shape of a giant apple.
(Hulton Archive/Harold Clements/Getty Images)

In America headache relief was available in the form of Emerson's Bromo-Seltzer, conceived in 1888. Captain Issac E Emerson developed the granular effervescent salt and sold it in distinctive blue glass bottles, also made by his company in Maryland. To help the Emerson Drug Co build customer awareness of its product packaging, and thus increase the chance of purchase when the consumer was next out shopping, the company built this giant replica bottle on a White truck in the 1920s to tour shopping areas and fairs.
(American Truck Historical Society)

Visitors to Blackpool sands in August 1935 certainly knew where to go for a much needed cup of tea. This fabulous teapot-shaped mobile kiosk was an instant attraction wherever it was displayed, and was also eco-friendly – being a horse-drawn vehicle.
(Hulton Archive/Fox Photos)

In 1936, Karl G Mayer, nephew of the Oscar Mayer hot dog and cold meats food company founder, had the idea of promoting the company's products by designing and building the Wienermobile™. The 13ft metal hot dog in the shape of an OSCAR MAYER® 'German Style Wiener', with open cockpits in the centre and rear of the vehicle, was built by General Body Company of Chicago, Illinois, at a cost of $5000, and was used to cruise downtown Chicago. As the company advertised, this was the world's first internal combustion hot dog! The Weinermobile™ evolved via five different versions between 1950 and 1954 on Dodge chassis by Gerstenslager of Wooster, Ohio. These vehicles had high-fidelity sound systems, and opening 'bun-roofs'. One of the original 1950s Weinermobile™ vehicles is now on display at the Henry Ford Museum in Dearborn, Michigan. (Oscar Meyer Division, Kraft Foods)

In 1958, a new vehicle design saw the introduction of the now familiar bubble-nose cockpit, which had the hot dog sat on a bun, rather than on a separate trailer. The new-look productmobile was based on a Willy's® Jeep chassis. Two further Wienermobile™ vehicles were built in 1969 by in-house OSCAR MAYER® mechanics at company headquarters in Madison, Wisconsin, and were used to tour foreign countries such as Japan and Spain. The vehicle bodies were made of glassfibre and Styrofoam, and were built on Chevy motorhome chassis with V6 engines. The design was replicated for the company in 1975 by Plastic Products of Milwaukee, using the same mould to fabricate the body. (Oscar Meyer Division, Kraft Foods)

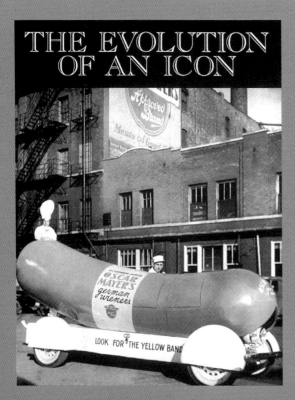

The design of the late 1960s/early 1970s vehicle seen here has been improved further to advertise the Yellow Band hot dogs and luncheon meats, and to assist in charity fundraising efforts. Today's fleet of eight Wienermobile™ vehicles covers around 1000 miles a week and is based on large GMC W series chassis, each 27ft long, 8ft wide, 11ft high, and weighing 14,050lb. Modern Weinermobile™ vehicles have gull-wing doors, the familiar OSCAR MAYER® rhomboid logo on the sides, relish-coloured upholstery on the six captain's chairs inside, and even hot dog-shaped dashboards and gloveboxes to complete the theme. Loudspeakers broadcast from an on-board radio station, including the jingle 'I wish I were an OSCAR MAYER Wiener', whilst steamers on the lower sides wafted the enticing aroma of freshly grilled hot dogs. Originally, promotional staff called 'Little Oscars (the world's smallest chefs)' distributed toys to children during promotions. Today's drivers are called 'Hotdoggers'. (George W Green/Oscar Meyer Division, Kraft Foods)

A team of salesmen launched the advertising campaign for the new Gleem Toothpaste in the 1960s by using a fleet of Messerschmitt three-wheel microcars. These quirky, yet innovative, small cars were the ideal platform on which to display larger-than-life tubes of toothpaste. With most new cars still relatively difficult to buy in the postwar era, these economical and diminutive 'bubble cars' became a frequent sight on Britain's roads, and from 1953 onward were sold by UK concessionaire, Cabin Scooters Ltd, London. (Hulton Archive/Thurston Hopkins/Getty Images)

The Outspan orange cars were based on a specially constructed chassis to give a 48in wheelbase. Running gear was from a BMC Mini, with a 998cc 4-cylinder Mini engine. At a time when apartheid in South Africa was a hugely sensitive issue politically and economically, these Outspan advertising vehicles were used to promote imported South African oranges and 'make things sweeter'. Here, two oranges squeeze together for a rare photo opportunity at The National Motor Museum, Beaulieu. (Motoring Picture Library, Beaulieu)

Braking or sharp cornering in one of the Outspan orange vehicles was not recommended since the top-heavy vehicles were extremely prone to rolling over. They were used mainly for promotional events though did see some street use, however. This particular vehicle's twin – now at the National Motor Museum, Beaulieu – has successfully completed a number of London-Brighton commercial vehicle runs in recent years.

The Outspan orange cars were so popular that a toy 'orange car' was made by Oxford Diecast in 1972, with the slogan 'the amazing Outspan orange' on the front.

THE AMAZING
Outspan
ORANGE

JUC 1

The Outspan Mini cars were built in 1972 by Brian Waite Enterprises Ltd, in Bodiam, Sussex. The bright orange cars have dimpled glassfibre bodies, orange vinyl seating for six people, padded roofs, orange-tinted windows, and can travel at 30mph. Over 200 pounds of ballast is built into the floor at the rear of the vehicles to prevent them rolling forward when braking hard. (Motoring Picture Library, Beaulieu)

HOB 446L

Access to the interior of the Outspan orange is through a door at the rear. The driver has a spoked steering wheel and plenty of instrumentation on the padded dashboard, including a speedometer, oil and temperature gauges, switches, and two very necessary air vents for cooling on warm days. (Motoring Picture Library, Beaulieu)

Lipsmackin', fuelswiggin', coolrollin', birdpullin', lightflashin', customtruckin' Pepsi Transit van was built by Al Llewelyn in 1977 as a promotional vehicle for Ford. The 5ft diameter giant can was rolled from 14swg metal in two pieces and joined, before being bolted to the Transit platform and sprayed in Pepsi livery. The interior sported a mirrored cocktail bar, custom deep-buttoned seating, shag-pile carpet, and disco lighting. The van is owned by the Ford Transit Heritage Collection. (Giles Chapman Library)

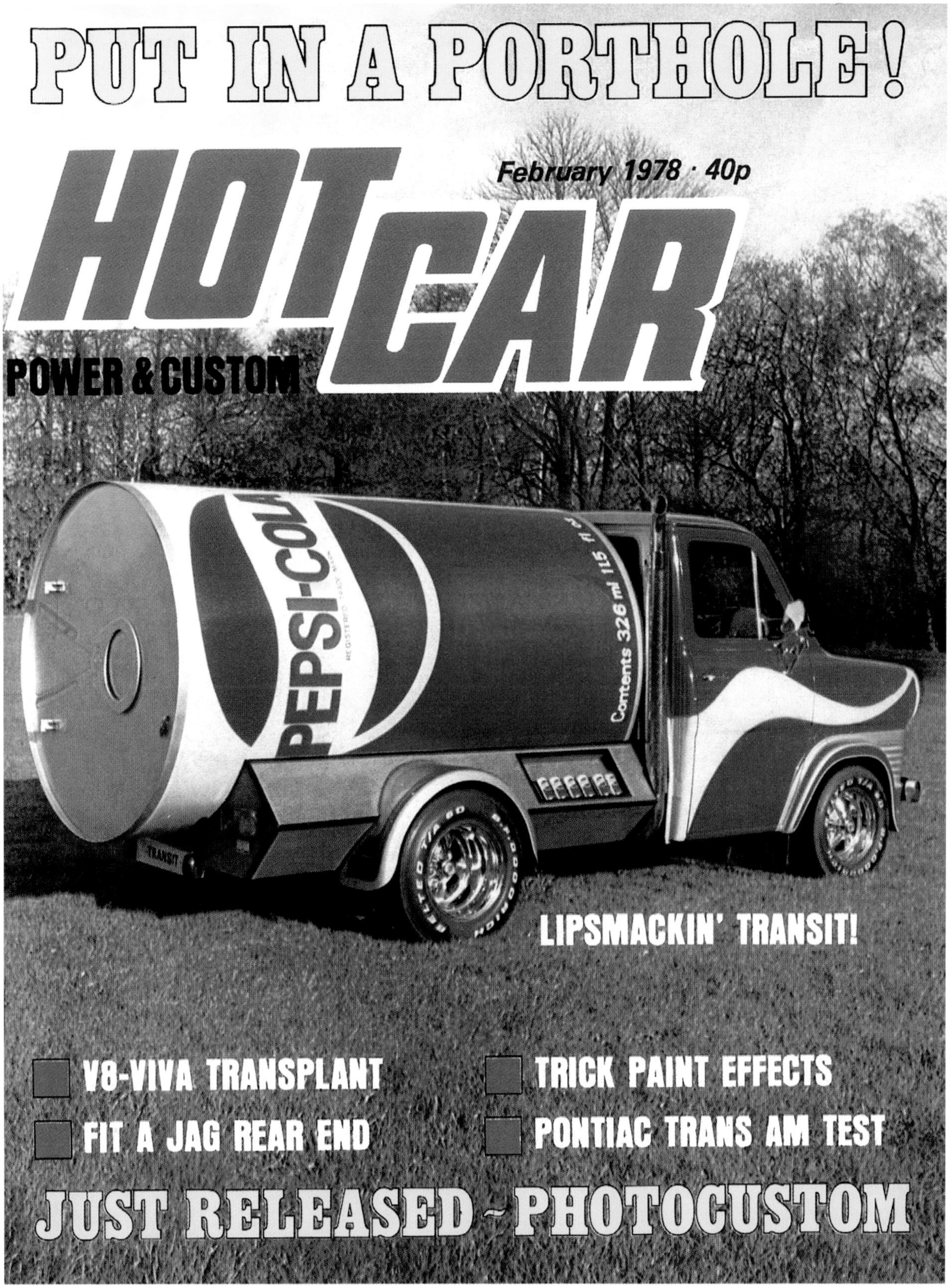

PUT IN A PORTHOLE!
HOT CAR
February 1978 · 40p
POWER & CUSTOM
PEPSI-COLA
Contents 326 ml 11.5 fl oz
TRANSIT
LIPSMACKIN' TRANSIT!
V8-VIVA TRANSPLANT
TRICK PAINT EFFECTS
FIT A JAG REAR END
PONTIAC TRANS AM TEST
JUST RELEASED ~ PHOTOCUSTOM

The February 1978 cover of Hot Car magazine featured the Ford Transit Pepsi van in all its glory. The 'ring-pull' can end is a door that swings open to reveal the sumptious interior. The vehicle was used both as an advertising vehicle at shows and a mobile office in which to conduct business. (*Hot Car*)

The VW Beetle has provided an ideal base for many productmobiles, with its independent chassis and rear-mounted, air-cooled engine. This 1970s example from the US has been fitted front and back with the ends of a giant hot dog to promote 'Mel's hot dogs'.

Named 'Clawde', this crustacean cruiser is the promotional vehicle for Red Lobster – a leading US chain of seafood diners founded in 1968 by Bill Darden. In the 1990s, the 25ft long, 11ft high and 8ft wide Clawde – made from glassfibre over a steel, wood and foam infrastructure, and weighing over 3000lb – was bolted to the top of a Ford F350 truck and toured the southeast of America to advertise Red Lobster's great-tasting seafood and 'Lobsterfests'. The 350 restaurants that comprised the Red Lobster chain were amalgamated into the Darden Restaurants Group in 1995, but still continue to provide one of America's finest seafood dining experiences.

Planters Nut Mobile van was created in 1999 as a way of advertising the famous peanut brand business founded by Amedeo Obici in 1906. The Nut Mobile is based on a GMC W-4 series truck chassis, featuring bright yellow peanut-shaped bodywork and giant 12ft high 'Mr Peanut' at the rear. The vehicle sports a dummy engine and 'blower' on the roof, whilst the real engine and four-speed automatic transmission are mounted on the chassis. Chrome exhaust pipes and 'moon' disc hubcaps give a custom look for its many appearances at auto shows and truck races. The vehicle also appeared at Macy's Thanksgiving Day Parade in 2002. The Mr Peanut figure has a camera fitted within his monocle which transmits onto a large screen TV to engage audience attention. (George W Green/Nabisco)

SPAM® (the pure pork shoulder and ham meat-in-a-tin) was introduced in 1937, and has remained popular ever since. To promote its products, between 2001 and 2002 the company introduced three SPAMMOBILE™ vehicles shaped like giant blue and yellow SPAM® tins. These vehicles are based on trolley car chassis, 28ft long, 8ft wide and 10ft high, and have pictures of the front of a SPAM® tin emblazoned on the sides, whilst the front has a friendly face with large eyes and a wide smile. The vehicles travel over 120,000 miles annually and are operated by SPAMbassadors preparing miniature SPAMBURGER hamburgers for testing at retail stores on weekdays, and concerts, festivals and sporting events at weekends. The SPAMMOBILES have full service mobile kitchens with electric sandwich grills used to prepare a total of 1.5m sandwiches at over 600 events each year. (Hormel Foods)

When they're not busy making their 'little tasty drinks' like smoothies, thickies and juicy waters, the folks at Innocent Drinks do up their vans to make them look innocent. The company has three Renault Kangoo vans, produced in 2002, called 'cow vans', complete with horns on the roof-mounted cooler, eyelashes over the lights, udders and tails. They even have a button which, when pressed, makes the cow 'moo'.
The first van is called Holly, and is a West London Longhorn, whilst the more recent addition to the company herd is Pat – a Lancashire Shorthorn with little horns to allow access into car parks with height restrictions. (Giles Chapman Library)

The company also has two DGVs (dancing grass vans) which visit events around the country. Fitted with loudspeakers and large smoothie bottles on the front, covered in grass and daisies on the outside and black and white cow-patterned interiors, the vans can 'dance' using a sophisticated hydraulics system fitted to each part of the suspension. (Innocent Drinks)

Red Bull energy drink may 'Give you wings', but this Mini definitely has its wheels on the ground and is carrying the can for the company, even though the car is privately owned. Finished in the colours of the drink's can, the silver and blue convertible also has the company's logo – featuring charging bulls – emblazoned on its sides.

Red Bull took up the mantle of producing promotional vehicles with the launch of its New Mini productmobiles in 2004. Built in Australia, a fleet of these semi-convertible Minis was constructed and fitted with large Red Bull cans mounted to a special platform on the rear deck. The vehicles are used throughout the summer months at outdoor and special promotional events. (Paul Wager)

New Minis weren't the only vehicles to get the Red Bull treatment. A fleet of New Beetles was converted to promote the drink in 2003/4. The sloping shape of the Beetle proved ideal on which to mount a large drinks can at the back, though it can't have done much for rear-view visibility!
(Neil Birkitt)

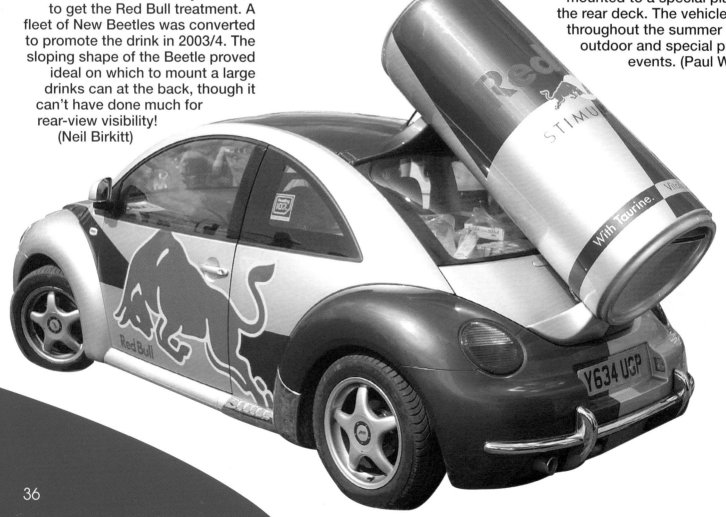

Chapter 2: *Only here for the beer*

A novelty of the 1906 Brewers' Exhibition was a 25hp Napier motor car with a Dutch Spyker chassis and body built to simulate an enormous bottle of Worthington Pale Ale. The vehicle, and a similar car, were laid up during the 1914-18 war, but restored to service in 1919 when they ran in populous centres – particularly in London. In 1921, two further 30hp Daimler Bottle cars with London registrations were added to the fleet. Each cost over £1000 to build; a considerable sum in those days. Two more were built for the company in 1923, including bottle car registration XU 177, now resident at the Coors Visitor Centre & Museum of Brewing. (Coors Visitor Centre & The Museum of Brewing, Burton upon Trent)

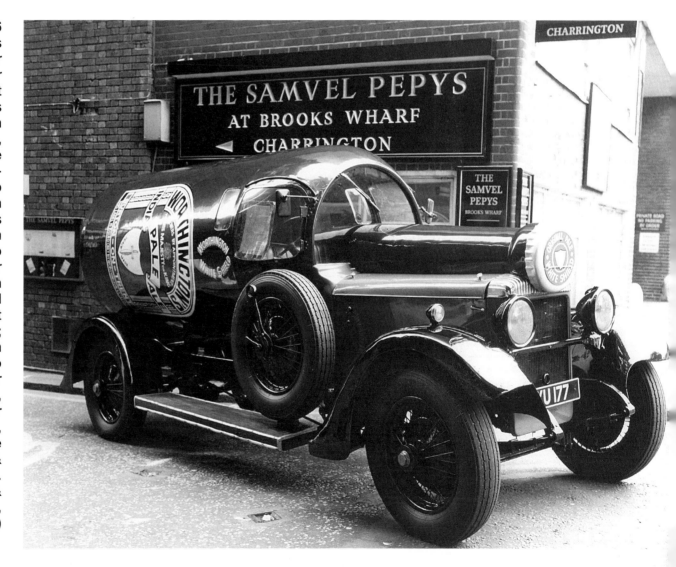

Bass, Ratcliff, and Gretton did not have bottle cars of their own, but after the 1927 merger with Worthington, the cars were shared and carried appropriate labels. They advertised either White Shield or Bass Pale Ale. The vehicles were built using 30hp Daimler TL 30 car chassis, transmissions and 6-cylinder engines supplied by Daimler Co of Coventry, minus bodies – a common practice during the 1920s. The bodies were made from boiler plate, and the complete vehicles weighed 2.3 tons. This photograph was taken in the 1960s. (Motoring Picture Library, Beaulieu)

Worthington bottle cars featured classic vintage Daimler controls: clutch pedal on the left, accelerator in the centre, and foot brake on the right. The gear lever – working a crash (non-synchromesh) gearbox – was on the right, operating in an external gate. There were four forward gears and one reverse. The handbrake was also on the right and operated on the transmission; pushed forward to apply and pulled back to release. Four-wheel braking was fitted to the cars. (Motoring Picture Library, Beaulieu)

Bottle car XT 5195 was given to the Montagu Motor Museum in the late 1950s after the Worthington vehicle fleet was modernised to meet more demanding traffic regulations. The bottle was finished in lustrous brown, whilst the chassis was a red flame colour. The museum, founded in 1952 by Lord Montagu, became the National Motoring Museum in July 1972. (Motoring Picture Library, Beaulieu)

The Worthington bottle car XU 177 was used for promotional purposes before being laid up during WWII. It re-emerged in 1946 with a Bedford engine. In the early 1950s, complaints from the police and the threat of the vehicles being taken off the road led to the necks being lowered sufficiently to improve the driver's view. The vehicle continued to work for the company until 1957 when it was sold into private ownership. It changed hands again in 1968, ending up at Charterhouse school, where it was worked on by the school motor club. It was subsequently bought back by Bass in 1971, and transferred to its home at the Museum of Brewing in 1977. (Coors Visitor Centre & The Museum of Brewing, Burton upon Trent)

Two of the three known surviving bottle cars were reunited during the Burton Festival in 1998, a gathering that concluded with the World Barrel Rolling Championships! Bottle car XU 177 was repainted to Worthington show condition for the festival. It is believed that a third vehicle resides in America, although this leaves two unaccounted for. However, it is likely that the Worthington car is in fact two vehicles, the result of cannibalisation in prewar days, when the intrinsic value of this collection of vehicles was not apparent. (Motoring Picture Library, Beaulieu)

The Daimler Bass bottle cars were replaced in 1957/58 by two large Seddon diesel motor bottles at a cost of £5300 the pair. More stringent traffic regulations prevented them running neck forward, so a different design was employed, with the driver sitting at the 'bottom' end of the glassfibre bottle with a clear forward view through a large area of windscreen.
(Coors Visitor Centre & The Museum of Brewing, Burton upon Trent)

This promotional delivery truck promoting Miller High Life – 'the Champagne of beers' – was owned by Buck Distributing Co Inc in the US during the 1950s. The base of the glassfibre bottle has a large windscreen fitted into it for driver visibility, whilst access is through a door at the side. (Classicphotos)

A Vins de France promotional vehicle at a display of coachbuilt vehicles at the Paris Salon in 1952. A huge basket of grapes and vat of wine are fitted to the upper part of the vehicle. (Redolfo Mailander/Ludvigsen Library)

Byrrh promoted its beers and spirits at the 1951 Paris Salon with this beer barrel-shaped vehicle. Note the bottle-shaped headlight housings; a particularly neat design touch. (Redolfo Mailander/Ludvigsen Library)

The Heineken Vatmobiles were used in the early 1960s for promotional purposes, and are still running today, used for special events. The wording on the side says *'wie in een Heineken vat zit verzuurt niet'*, a variant of an old Dutch proverb which roughly translates as 'Whoever is in the Heineken barrel will not turn sour'. (Heineken Collection, Amsterdam)

The Heineken beer barrel-shaped Vatmobile was constructed on a DAF car chassis fitted with a 'flat' 2-cylinder, 600cc air-cooled engine and Variomatic running gear. This was the belt-driven forerunner of today's CVT gearboxes with one forward and one reverse 'speed', there being no clutch, clutch pedal or gearlever. The variable drive was taken to the rear wheels by stepless toothed rubber belts in a V-formation. This efficient system was perfect for an oddball vehicle like the mobile barrel. (Heineken Collection, Amsterdam)

This GUINNESS® branded carnival float was provided for a local event in 1959. The GUINNESS Exports Ltd flatbed lorry has been decorated with funfair swings and promotional bottles, and carries the message 'Carnival time is GUINNESS time' on its flanks. (Diageo. The word GUINNESS and HARP device are trade marks)

GUINNESS® stout beer is stacked high in crates on this GUINNESS Exports Ltd lorry seen in Liverpool in the early 1960s. The lorries, whilst not shaped like bottles, carried large bottle branding above and next to the driver's cab. (Diageo)

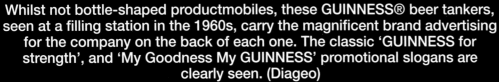

Whilst not bottle-shaped productmobiles, these GUINNESS® beer tankers, seen at a filling station in the 1960s, carry the magnificent brand advertising for the company on the back of each one. The classic 'GUINNESS for strength', and 'My Goodness My GUINNESS' promotional slogans are clearly seen. (Diageo)

Photographed near the St James Gate brewery, this GUINNESS® beer truck is heading for a continental destination, judging by the 'EC consignee' designation on the side.

GUINNESS® branded Minivans were destined for promotional work in the US in the early 1960s. Seen here in Liverpool before departure from the port, on their roofs the Minivans feature GUINNESS beer bottles, globes, and the company's figurine. (Diageo)

Built in 1918 on a Dodge truck chassis, this productmobile is promoting well-known confectionery brand, Pep-O-Mint Life Savers candies in the US. The sweets were advertised as a 'dainty confection' by the manufacturer, Mint Products Co. The driver sat behind the round window in the vehicle centre from where forward visibility must have been severely restricted. The Pep-O-Mint brand is now owned by the Nabisco Foods Group of RJR Nabisco.
(Nabisco Foods Group, RJR Nabisco/George W Green)

Mr & Mrs Russell Stover began a candy business in their bungalow home in Denver, Colorado, in 1923. Mr Stover was the salesman, whilst Mrs Stover actually made the products, marketed originally as 'Mrs Stover's Bungalow Candies'. Being a cottage industry, a custom-built 'bungalow store' delivery truck was ordered from Dodge in 1925, complete with flower boxes and smoking chimney, and used to promote and sell the candies throughout the midwest in 1926. This excellent recreation of the original vehicle is still in operation with the company, which is now the number one seller of boxed chocolate brands in America, and the largest producer of hand-dipped chocolates in the world.
(Russell Stover Candies/George W Green)

Pep-O-Mint Life Savers Candy Roll car from the late 1920s features an open-topped convertible design with improved seating comfort and better visibilty. The vehicle still took the shape of the product – a roll of candies – and carried a message on the side saying 'Candy mint with the hole'.
(Hulton Archive/Getty Images)

This mouthwatering promotional vehicle advertising 'Ye Olde Guernsey Sweet Shoppe', established in 1879, was built on a 1932/33 Bedford 12cwt chassis and used on the island to promote the confectionery shop. Pascalls sweets were advertised on the rear doors of this cute mobile house, which was built by R J Collins & Co. (Motoring Picture Library, Beaulieu)

William Barg and Fred Foster created the Barg & Foster Candy company in Milwaukee, Wisconsin, in 1918 as a wholesale candy distributor. They also became candy bar makers in 1923 when they bought out the Sperry Candy Co, and introduced confectionery such as the 'Chicken Dinner' and the 'Denver Sandwich'. State laws required manufacturers and distributors to hold different licenses and names, so the Sperry Candy Co operated two companies within the same building: wholesale on the first floor, and manufacture of candy bars and nut rolls on the second, third and fourth floors. Fleets of Sperry promotional chicken wagons were used to advertise and deliver the products. This example from the war years carries the message 'Eat a Chicken Dinner and see behind German Lines'. (Tom Torrans)

Sperry's animated Chicken Dinner wagons were based on Ford F-100 pickup trucks, and were a regular sight on the roads in the early 1950s. The vehicle number was painted on the door. These mobile chicken adverts were an important part of Sperry's nickel candy bar promotions, and the chicken wagons would cackle and crow for added effect when the horn was pushed. Here, three Chicken Dinner vehicles are seen outside a store promoting the product. A similar company float was used in parades, and the vehicles were also featured on postcards of the time. Sperry was bought out by Pearsons Candy Co in 1962. (Tom Torrans)

The Chicken Dinner candy bar was so called because it was introduced in the era of the American Great Depression (1929-1941), when the President was promising the people they would have 'chicken in every pot'. The nourishing candy bar had nuts in it which provided protein, like chicken, as well as caramel and chocolate. (Tom Torrans)

The Denver Sandwich bars were promoted with Ford trucks shaped like a covered wagon, often towing a covered wagon trailer. The promotional face of the advertising was a character called Denver Ike, and his mule, Mike, who featured on the fabric of the wagon and poster advertising of the time. Here, the vehicle is parked outside a local Ford parts and accessories distributor in the late 1940s/early 1950s. (Tom Torrans)

Taken in front of the Sperry Candy Co factory in the late 1920s/early 1930s, this amazing composite photo shows the complete fleet of cars, jeeps and trucks lined up and ready for action delivering Chicken Dinner candy bars across the state. (Tom Torrans)

A chocolate lover's delight! Cadbury Schweppes plc commissioned the construction of three Cadbury Creme Egg cars in the late 1980s to promote the fondant-filled chocolate eggs at the Cadbury World visitor centre in Birmingham, and at regional events around the country during the key selling time for the product between New Year and Easter. (Cadbury Schweppes plc/V4 Design Studio)

The Creme Egg cars were based on the chassis of Bedford Rascal vans, registered in 1988/1989. Fitted with glassfibre bodies, their extreme curvature required that the vehicle's foot control pedals be re-aligned, making them very difficult to drive. Only those who were contortionists or had very small feet found them comfortable! (Cadbury Schweppes plc/V4 Design Studio)

Front view of one of the Creme Egg cars shows the heavy branding for the product on a shape that perfectly replicates the foil-wrapped chocolate item. Lighting at the front is courtesy of Citroën 2CV headlights mounted on specially-shaped brackets, which also form supports for the very necessary large rear-view mirrors. (Cadbury Schweppes plc/V4 Design Studio)

Entry and exit from the egg is courtesy of an
upward-lifting side door, assisted by large gas
rams. (Cadbury Schweppes plc/V4 Design Studio)

An egg on a roll! Even the wheel trims and headlight bowls are branded with the Creme Egg yellow chick.
(Cadbury Schweppes plc/V4 Design)

The panoramic windscreens of the Creme Egg cars were especially made to fit the curvature of the glassfibre bodies, and had windscreen wipers adapted from commercial vehicles to give a clean sweep. (Cadbury Schweppes plc/V4 Design Studio)

It's no yoke – even Cadbury couldn't resist attaching vehicle 'bumper stickers' to the cars. 'You should see the bird that laid this', 'Painted in eggshell finish', and 'My other car is a Mini-Egg' should be enough to 'crack up' other drivers following these unique vehicles. (Cadbury Schweppes plc/V4 Design Studio)

Such was the popularity of the Cadbury Creme Egg cars that in 1993 diecast makers, Corgi, produced a toy version of the vehicles. The red and blue plastic toy car was produced exclusively for Cadbury and sold at Cadbury World.

The first of Hershey's Kissmobile cruisers was built in 1997 to celebrate the 90th anniversary of Hershey's Kisses brand chocolates; a second followed in 1999. Both are built on GMC W-4, W-series truck chassis with V8 engines. Rolling monuments to the perennially popular foil-clad milk chocolates, each vehicle has a huge, 8-foot tall silver-coated glassfibre Kiss at the front (the driver's cockpit), and either a gold foil 'Kiss with Almonds' in the centre and striped 'Hugs' at the rear, or a 'Caramel Kiss' and 'Dark' chocolate Kiss combination. (Hershey Food Corp)

The Kissmobiles resemble three giant Hershey's chocolates, and are used on tours annually to promote the confectionery. The centre Kiss is equipped with a 42in plasma screen television, a DVD and sound system complete with karaoke system to entertain visitors with games and contests during sampling, and there is a crew of two 'chocolate ambassadors per vehicle. The back 'Hug' compartment is a refrigerator holding 230,000 Hugs and Kisses. (Hershey Food Corp)

Prototype Source Inc of Santa Barbara, California, took six months to design and build the original 26-ft long Hershey's Kissmobile. Each vehicle travels more than 50,000 miles annually on 60-city trips to reach consumers at supermarkets, fairs and sporting events. Part of the Kissmobile's mission is to visit children's hospitals and support the Children's Miracle Network, a charity for which Hershey's and its employees have raised $5m since 1987. (Hershey Food Corp)

Cadbury used the biggest street-legal monster truck (8ft tall, 20ft long) around shopping centres in the UK in 2005 to promote sampling of its Cadbury Giant Fingers biscuits. The vehicle was built by Monster Truck Racing in Northants. (MTR Promotions Ltd)

Based on a Toyota Hilux pickup, the Cadbury Monster Truck is a 4WD vehicle with a difference! Sporting a huge wrapped chocolate finger biscuit on the rear deck, and plenty of fresh air underneath, the truck is used to promote the product at public events, where customers can win boxes of the chocolate delight. (MTR Promotions Ltd)

Giant Fingers call for a giant promotional vehicle, and the monster truck is an ideal base for some unmissable Cadbury advertising out on the streets, and at sampling venues across the country. (MTR Promotions Ltd)

Chapter 4: *Leisure, pleasure and power pop*

In 1918, just after the end of WWI, George Rowney & Co, pencil manufacturer, used this specially-constructed Mercedes-Benz 'pencil van' for metropolitan deliveries of its pencils and art materials. The company was based in offices in Percy Street, London, and the productmobile was an early attempt to introduce modern marketing methods to the family business, founded in 1789. Note the royal patronage on the vehicle's side. (Giles Chapman Library)

Stepping out in style is this 'shoe car' built for Daniel Neal Children's Shoemakers on a 1921 Ford Model T chassis and with coachwork by Riverside Motor Works. The message on the side reads 'PHAT PHEET'. Looking back at this early promotional vehicle we can only assume that this was the brand of shoes being advertised!
(Motoring Picture Library, Beaulieu)

Whilst supply problems with all luxury goods during the war kicked the beautiful game into touch, this British manufacturer of sports and games was delighted to tell prospective purchasers and sports players that there was now good news as 'There will be more British sports boots in 1947'. This Bedford GSV lorry from Blue Star Garages provided the platform to advertise football boots in 1946. (Motoring Picture Library, Beaulieu)

If the shoe fits, drive it! Here, a VW Beetle chassis and running gear provides the rolling stock for a giant football boot car. This South American vehicle even has domed hubcaps painted like footballs. Clearly, the driver is quite happy to put his best foot forward ...

This 'Shoemobile' from California shows that boots aren't just made for walking whilst out promoting Quality Shoe Service of Santa Monica. Shaped like a boot, the vehicle was based on Honda mechanicals with a motorcycle engine, and also had the license plate 'Boot'. (Quality Shoe Service/ George W Green)

There's not much room in the boot of this giant pink shoe, built in 2004 on a 1000cc motor tricycle. The vehicle is used in Marikina, east of Manila, to boost the image of shoes made in the city in the face of cheap Chinese imports. At least if they break down, they won't need a 'toe' … (Reuters)

And you thought luggage on wheels was a recent phenomenon.

Fine luggage since 1839. Located at 400 Madison Ave. at 48th St., New York. 212-755-5888.

And you thought luggage on wheels was a recent phenomenon? This productmobile in the shape of a giant trunk advertises the fact that Crouch & Fitzgerald on Madison Avenue, New York, made fine luggage for 150 years since 1839. (George W Green)

Zippo introduced its famous windproof lighter with a lifetime guarantee in 1932, and advertised the product by driving a specially-constructed 'Zippo Car' across all US states in 1947. The whereabouts of this car is unknown but, in 1998, an exact replica was constructed, built on a 1947 Chrysler Saratoga New Yorker chassis. The vehicle features two Zippo lighters forming a central custom-made cab, with tops that open and close realistically making up the roof. Removable neon 'flames' can be attached for added effect, and are stowed in the cab whilst travelling. The two-door cab has the word 'Zippo' etched in 24 carat gold plate lettering on the side. This unique vehicle is on permanent display at the Zippo/Case visitor's Centre in Pennsylvania. (Zippo Manufacturing Co/George W Green)

Given the availability in the early 1950s of mass-market 'luxury' consumer goods like cameras, and the burgeoning holiday market, there was never a better time to take photographs. In June 1951, cars with cameras mounted on their roofs were used to advertise a *Picture Post* photography competition with the slogan 'Post your pictures to Picture Post'.
(George Konig/Hulton Archive/Getty Images)

TUNE·IN & TURN·ON
THE VOX·MOBILE!

'Tune In & Turn On to the Voxmobile' proclaims this period print advertisement. Vox guitars and amplifiers were given a huge boost by the use of this amazing productmobile on TV shows, films and at fairs across the US in 1968. Originally styled as the 'Vox Kart', the George Barris-built vehicle cost a cool $30,000 to construct.

THE VOXMOBILE — the fastest guitar in the country! You are looking at a dream car that not only travels 175 mph but also turns on! An entire rock 'n roll band can plug in to this vehicle and play through its amplifiers. There is a dual manual continental organ mounted in the rear deck. Also, there are 32 guitar jack inputs all around the car, allowing musicians to play on every side for a 360-degree happening! Hidden in the framework of the car are five 12" speakers and tweeters, an 18" bass speaker, and two main driver speakers. The total power output is rated close to 1000 peak watts! Sound balances are controlled from the dashboard. The high performance 289 cu. in. Ford Cobra engine delivers the power to the rear wheels through a special transmission. The VOXMOBILE is headed for stardom! It is appearing on national TV shows, in motion pictures, automobile shows and teenage fairs across the country! Look for it in your city!

VOX GUITARS AND AMPLIFIERS

A DIVISION OF THOMAS ORGAN CO., 8345 HAYVENHURST, SEPULVEDA, CALIF. 91343

· THOMAS ORGAN CO   1968   PRINTED IN U.S.A   08-41008-0

Wonderfully period Voxmobile promotional shot, taken in the late 1960s at the height of psychedelia and clothes boutiques.

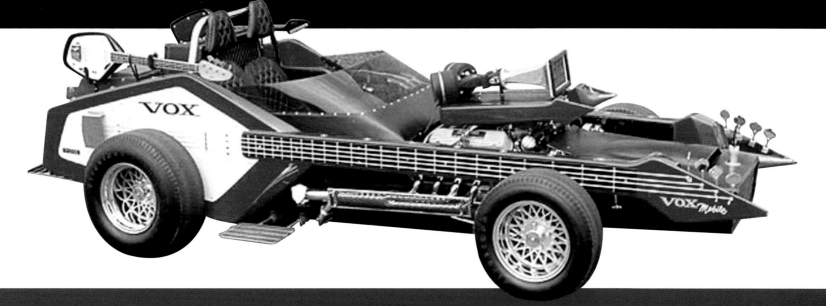

The Voxmobile, commissioned in 1967 by Warren Hampton of the Vox Guitar Company, was created by customiser George Barris in 1968. The two-seat roadster 'guitar car' was designed not only to generate media attention with its metalflake red and pearl white-painted, guitar-profiled body complete with frets, strings and tuning keys, but also work as a fully-functioning, driveable vehicle. What's more, it could be a completely self-contained rolling soundstage, incorporating an operational Vox continental organ, three Vox Beatle amplifiers, five 12in speakers and tweeters, an 18in bass speaker, two main driver speakers, and 32 guitar jacks. Total power output was rated at 1000 watts. (George Barris)

The Voxmobile appeared on the TV show *Groovy* with host Mike Blodgett and the band Strawberry Alarm Clock on Venice Beach. The vehicle also appeared on the TV quiz show *Dialing for Dollars*, at trade displays, and even at hot rod and auto shows across the US. (George Barris)

The fastest guitar in the country was an album released in 1968 by ace county session guitarist, Jimmy Bryant. The album cover featured the Voxmobile, and tracks included one entitled *Voxwagon*.

The Voxmobile appeared in many advertisements with Jimmy Bryant, a session musician with the nickname 'the world's fastest guitarist'. A Ford Cobra 289 V8 powerplant allowed the Barris creation to travel at speeds of up to 175mph. A Ford automatic transmission, a hot rod-style chassis with a chromed drop tube axle at the front, coil spring rear suspension with Ford 9in rear axle, and Rader wheels shod with Firestone tyres completed the ensemble. (George Barris)

Under promotional contract to use Vox products when the Voxmobile was originally built, musician Jimmy Bryant was an ideal frontman for the company. The Voxmobile emitted wild guitar sounds complete with reverb, treble/bass and mid-range boost from its integral amplifiers, and the special chrome steps mounted astride the body allowed three guitarists to play music whilst the car was driven in a parade. (George Barris)

THE CHURCHMOBILE
— IRELAND'S CHURCH·ON·WHEELS —

Ireland's church-on-wheels, the Churchmobile, was operated between 1972 and 1984 by the only rural Baptist gathering in Ireland, established in 1882. The outside was finished in an attractive Gothic design complete with foldaway spire. The interior was designed to provide maximum seating space, and lighting was provided by mains electricity and an additional battery-powered system for emergency use. It was drawn by Kenneth Bromley for a greetings card. (Pastor Robert Dunlop)

The Churchmobile was built from a converted single-deck Leyland bus in Dublin in 1972, and retained the original body and chassis. Cost of construction was about £3000. It had a portable pulpit, electronic organ, seated 30-35 people, and was operated by the Rev Robert Dunlop, Baptist minister at Brannockstown, Co Kildare, Republic of Ireland. The church-on-wheels was used for services and meetings, and to display and sell Bibles and religious literature over a wide area. (Pastor Robert Dunlop)

Par for the course was this Land Rover golf ball development machine produced by British Leyland, Solihull, in the 1970s. The aptly-shaped signage on the side of the vehicle, and fold down machine says 'Penfold patented'. Was it a big hit with the golfers, we wonder, or just another handicap in the turbulent era of British car factory strikes? (Giles Chapman Library)

Motorised advertising vehicles developed in the early 20th century with many delivery vans and lorries sign-written to promote a company's products. Cars and motorcycles were less common as motorised advertisements, but some – such as this early example for Triumph Motorcycles – proved that anything was possible, even on two wheels.
(Motoring Picture Library, Beaulieu)

This Levis 'Castrol' bike from Wakefield adds another dimension to the possibilities of product advertising by touring the streets complete with a sidecar in the shape of a square Castrol XL can. The bike may well have been used by a local garage to promote the oil company's goods. (Motoring Picture Library, Beaulieu)

A 'Chock Full o'Nuts novelty truck promoting the smooth, but slightly nutty, American coffee that originated in New York city over 70 years ago. The period promotional vehicle was shaped like a cabin with a screened-in porch, and is seen here parked outside the Corn Exchange Bank Trust Company, New York, in January 1940. In 1964 J Lyons & Co acquired an interest in the Chock Full o' Nuts Corporation in USA from the Beechnut Company, to add to its other coffee brands. The Chock Full o'Nuts brand has been owned by food giant Sara-Lee since 2000, and has recently undergone a national advertising promotion. (Hulton Archive/ Getty Images)

This miniature house on the back of a car is a mobile advertisement for a Sacremento lumber and construction company in the US called Cuttermill. The photograph was taken on 26th June 1924, and shows the ingenuity of companies promoting their services at a time when money in Depression-hit America was tight, and productmobiles were recognised as a great way to attract business. (Hulton Archive/Topical Press Agency/Getty Images)

Swedish Viking Sparkplug Car from 1925 was used to promote racing plugs. The car was registered as a 'Pope-Minerva', with the chassis from a Pope, but powered by a Minerva engine. The car featured a thin metal sparkplug on the radiator cap, and discs to hide the wooden spoked wheels. The text on the cowl says 'Viking Sparkplugs, completely detachable, all parts exchangeable, Swedish invention, Swedish production'. The car was probably scrapped around 1930. The Viking factory still exists today as BACHO, making saw blades. (Roland Swälas)

Parked outside a Goodyear tyre and Kendall motor oil sales outlet in the US, this 1930s Goodyear car is a stretch limousine with a difference. Pulling a huge Goodyear tyre mounted to the back of the car, it could hardly be missed! (Classicphotos)

Taken in 1935, this photograph shows the same stretch automobile pulling the oversize Goodyear tyre behind it. The message on the side of the vehicle says 'World's Largest Tire built by Goodyear. Looking forward to the future'. (Hulton Archive/Historic Photo Archive/Getty Images)

This 1956 Armco Drainage and Metal Products 'Steelmobile' truck was shaped like a giant section of drainage piping. Armco used the vehicle as a demonstration unit and conference venue, reaching contractors, officials and engineering students in 28 different colleges as it toured the US and Canada on an 18 month, 50,000 mile tour, taking in major cities served by its 50 fabricating plants. The vehicle took nine months to build and the body was made of stainless steel. The side door was electrically operated and also served as a canopy; steps allowed entry to the exhibition area inside the elliptical body. (Henry Elrod/George W Green)

One car that should never have needed a bump start was the Chloride battery car, built as a promotional vehicle for the company in 1975. The very angular body was built onto Hillman Imp underpinnings, and with the standard rear water-cooled engine. (Motoring Picture Library, Beaulieu)

Launched in 1995 in conjunction with British Motor Heritage, the Duckhams Heritage range of oils included an engine oil blended to the original Q20-50 formula, especially to suit engines of the 1950s and '60s. Here, the Duckhams Q Car is pictured in matching livery at the Heritage Museum, Gaydon. (Duckhams)

Duckhams Q Car was built by Austin Morris at BL's Longbridge works, and is owned by the British Motor Industry Heritage Trust, Gaydon. It has appeared in different liveries and, for the Queen's Silver Jubilee in May 1977, the Q Car (fitted with a special Silver Jubilee medallion) toured the country to promote the oil sold in special cartons carrying the Union Flag. The 'Mini-Can' car is seen here with well-known *Multi-Coloured Swap Shop* television presenter, Keith Chegwin. (Motoring Picture Library, Beaulieu)

This experimental car, named the 'Illusion buggy', was built by Dave Puhl to promote Petersen Publishing Company's exhibition in 1966 at the New York International Automobile Show. It took three years to build and is a single-seater with a hand-formed aluminium body, 289 cubic inch Ford V8 engine, and V-shaped handlebar in place of a conventional steering wheel. The model is Brigitte Eichenauer, a former Miss Frankfurt and Hollywood television actress.
(Giles Chapman Library)

The Sonic, built in 1981 by hot rodder Nick Butler for Wolfrace Wheels, was a promotional vehicle for the company's new 'pepperpot' wheels, soon to appear on the Ford XR2. Built around a custom-made tubular steel space frame, and with one-piece futuristic glassfibre bodywork, Sonic used twin Rover 3.5 litre V8 engines with Holley carburettors producing around 250bhp each. Top speed of the street legal car was around 150mph. Sonic was fitted with six of the new wheels, four standard production 13in wheels at the front, and two specially cast 15in wheels at the rear. (Wolfrace)

The futuristic styling of Sonic was matched by advanced engineering. Computers kept the two engines in synchronisation, with similarly controlled automatic transmissions. The braking system was similar to that used on the Tyrell 6-wheeled Formula 1 cars of the era, and the car had proper Ackerman steering to all front four wheels. Here, pop singer Wolfie Witcher, complete with spanner, uses Sonic to promote his latest record. (Giles Chapman Library)

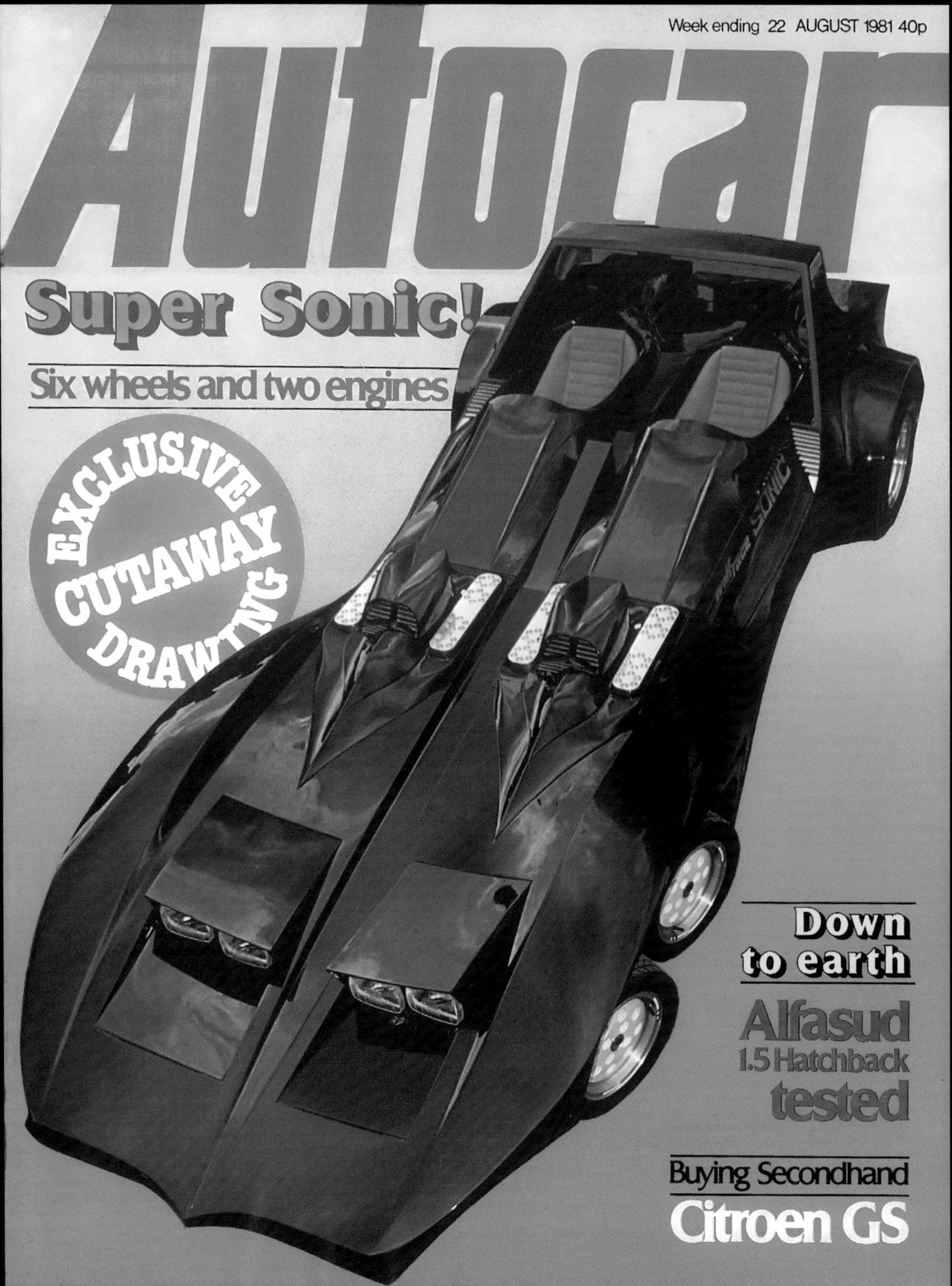

Week ending 22 AUGUST 1981 40p

Autocar

Super Sonic!

Six wheels and two engines

EXCLUSIVE CUTAWAY DRAWING

Down to earth

Alfasud 1.5 Hatchback tested

Buying Secondhand Citroen GS

Autocar magazine from August 1981 featured the six-wheeled and twin-engined 'Super Sonic', including a revealing cutaway drawing showing what lay beneath Sonic's styling skin.

Land Rover has a reputation for strength and go-anywhere potential with its military-style 4x4s, which explains why the company was chosen to supply vehicles for the 1995 Hollywood comic book movie, *Judge Dredd*, starring Sylvester Stallone. The futuristic and angular 'City Cab' Land Rovers were created purely as specials for use in the film. (Giles Chapman Library)

A productmobile with a difference! UK insurance company, Direct Line, introduced the famous red telephone on wheels to promote its products in the 1980s. Large scale (non-motorised) promotional versions of the telephone appeared at exhibitions around the country, whilst a working version of the telephone could be bought by diehard collectors. A child's version of the red telephone was also produced by toy company, Matchbox.

Index

Bibliography

Special Use Vehicles: An illustrated history of unconventional cars and trucks worldwide; Green, George W McFarland & Company Inc, Jefferson, North Carolina, 2003. www.mcfarlandpub.com